Rings And Emeralds

Harine A.L

BookLeaf Publishing

India | USA | UK

Presentation by *BookLeaf Publishing*

Web: www.bookleafpub.com

E-mail: info@bookleafpub.com

ISBN: 9789363315259

First edition 2024

DEDICATION

I dedicate this book to my parents, whom I'm blessed to have, for I shall be forever in debt for the love and affection I've been showered upon.

ACKNOWLEDGEMENT

Poems provide a subjective experience for readers, giving rise to a plethora of interpretations bound by their emotions.

I express my deepest gratitude to the almighty for giving me the strength and knowledge to write this book.

Most importantly, I thank my family and friends for their continued support and encouragement.

PREFACE

Poems are the embodiments of one's emotions and imagination that seep deep into channels of our chambers whose rhythm remains divine while in search of a belief to hold on to.

Being an earthly endeavor of divine origin I welcome the readers on this journey of having to experience the elegance and beauty of love.

Heartfelt Whispers

Thy warmth comforts me on cold winter
mornings
while thy arms wrap around me in mother's
disguise.

I wake up to the sound of thy heartbeat that
rhythms with mine
Creating the song of our love that cannot be
heard
But, only seen and felt when I look into thy
eyes.

A Walk of Empyreal Sight

Walking down the sunset boulevard
Our hands clasped while,
Our lives entwined.

Withered flowers of
Our now blossomed life soon
Turned to life in thy heart.

Nuzzled and cuddled by the warmth
While the stars shined the brightest
Dimming the moon they shine
Just as my eyes did at thy sight.

The Rhythm of Love

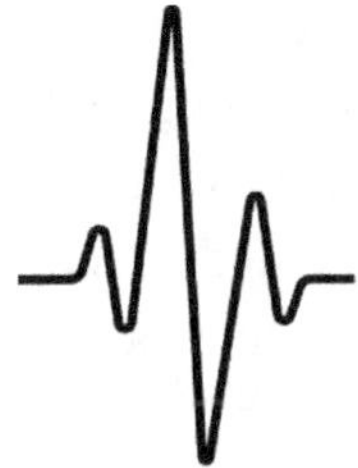

Twilight's warmth stretched
While cold zephyr swept beside.
Heartfelt beatings, resonating
Through the entwined boughs,
Of what were once sprigs.

Flares of red, tears of sap,
Flawed and unraveled, while
The arms froze in agony.

Where the blossomed withered
Began, an era of the tenebrific reality.
Realms energized through thoughts of a distant
past,
Devouring the lucency, a twin,
A mirage arising from a faux beacon
Of love and hope.
Looking through the ephemeral life,

Scars of a pain, inexorable,
Only to realize, "It was all just a dream."

While trails blurred by boundless darkness,
Hands reached for the arms ticked again,
Sheltering the lonely longing heart,
Soothing burns far beyond reach.
The dawning promise of Venus kept,
Reviving the faded innocence,
Ivory in disguise,
Anything but despise.

Forever A Wish

What were once merged,
Submerged in dread for,
Finding themselves torn apart
Across oceans it meant.

But what was it that it truly led to?
The untold truth of the wrongly guarded,
The greatest of lesions in the 'unbreakable'
Unlike, was it what we wished it to be?

A trust unlike any,
The hope wished by many,
A love dreamt upon by every,
Every awakened heart found beating…

A Supernal Vision

Grasses drenched, leaves submerged,
For love was left never unturned,
Canopies of warmth in the lands of heart,
Lost in thy sight, a selfless art.

Lands stretched to the never-ending stars,
While thy beaming radiance struck my heart.

Withered flowers of winter mornings,
Soon began blooming in bliss,
For love emerged, alive and nurtured,
While strings of love bound together.

An Eternal Saviour

Lurking in the dark, souls cloaked in agony,
While hearts throbbed for closure.
Love swaddling the children of god,
For if life was to be immortal,
It was all to remain.
Ebullient radiance extirpating the Stygian,
Unraveling the misery entwined for eons.
The winged souls of a newborn era
Soaring high, having found its raison d'être.
Though not sought by many,
Love is a blessing unlike any.

An Endless Shine

Tracing paths to a never-ending past
Gazing thy sight a prisoner of thy heart
Racing hearts like tide under the moon
Forever lost in your endless shine.

Elemental Mails of Love

Amidst the setting sky of the vast blue,
Where waves spoke of distant lovers,
While the wind sang of the ethereal,
Castles of sand rose beyond the tide,
While thrones of woven threads entwined the
hearts,
Swells submerged, while the moon rose,
Illuminating the darkness, the knight in cold.

Beloved are Thy!

Flickering lights of the burning embers
Fireflies of the night in thy heather-filled
chambers

Setting sun of distant moors
Scintillating stars of moonless sky
Scented flowers of the eternal night
Stare in reverence for thy yearning
My beloved!

Accidental Mozzle

Mends made in tideless seas
While the heaven's blues closed in closure
Maidens of heaven longed for thy sight
While mortal I was endowed with thy.

Laid thy sight like soft whispers of breeze
While thy faint blush tinted the sky
Cradled my soul like the serape of the west
While thy arms raised my sunken heart.

The Victory in the Lost

Dimming sky lit up at thy sight
While thy cheeks blushed like twilight
Birds desirous of thy dulcet tone
While stars glisten in admiration

The soul of dawn's first dew
A heart birthed by Venus herself
Turning maidens of heaven covetous
For thy paint my embers of love whole

While I stare at thy in reverence
Lost in thy eyes of endless ardor
Yet victorious in love.

Forever Lovers

A known soul yet an unfamiliar face
The warmth of my mother
But the body of a stranger

Thy walk across is disguise
Though my heart recognized
With years shall I realize

For my love
Meant to be, we are
Forever lovers.

Within Winds An Arcana

Sunny was it, but misty was my mind,
Directions unknown, yet felt by my,
Hard chest poundings that beat like the wind
On the window shields during cold winter
nights.

A shadow in the dark, fading away in the lights,
Lifting of my darkness I see within thy eyes,
The warmth I'd felt in my mother's loving arms,
Never recreated, not until now.

Was it the blue sky? Or the green lands?
Your eternal love? Or your ever-beating heart?

Lifted didn't it, my spirit up high,
And gave me a chance to give life a try.

Didn't I realize? For life was it,
Didn't I relish? For love was it,
Didn't I require? For your warmth it is,
That truly comforts while the eternal winds
Blow through your life,
Yet thy are left unshaken with time.

Forever A Fantasy

Mild chirrups of Monday blues
Replaced by thy heart's rhythm.
An infant in mother's arm
Or is that what I'd like to feel it as?

Warm and secure is thy voice
Just as thy soul is.

Now I shall wake up to it
For long gone were the chirrups
And no longer did they remain
Forever a fantasy.

Venus's First Born

Dawn hit thy lands
While the winds sang of thy warmth
The birds chirped of thy love
While flowers bloomed in thy radiance.

An ethereal sight of Cupid himself
The true heir of love herself
Venus's firstborn
The soul whose love I'd longed.

A Prayer

Distant hearts in arms reach
Charismatic eyes making a breach
Quarrels loomed and turned to leech
Yet love is all I wish to preach.

Masked Ain't Thy?

Belie, Oh my!
For radiant are thy
Diving beyond thy warm eyes
A world of deep-sea vents.

Resting beneath the eternal crest
While enamored at thy beatific sight
An eternal whisper of
The enchanted heart!

Godsent Aren't Thy?

How'd I not admire?
For ain't thy radiant?
From beneath the chambers of Stygian
Shone thy turning the lifeless to rhythms.

Crossing leagues for a glimpse
While struck ain't I in reverence
For thy a sight of worldly grace
And within thy I sought solace.

To Thy, Almighty!

They say,
Till death do us part
Yet then do we stay merged

Awaiting for thy presence
My bijou heart tears for thy
For united in prayer, my love
For thy, I remain entwined in reverence

A sight so divine
For my soul shall revive
All the nocturnes in the dark
Yet thy shall be my light

Obeisance shall remain infinite for thy
While my soul is an oblation for thy
Thy benevolent sight shall break the sky
For thy in it is for us to realize

Yet for thy I whisper in prayer
Though who may bewitch my heart
Thy shall and always be its true master.

In Gloom Thy Shall Return

Muzzy whispers cloaked the minds
Conjuring the Stygian of moonless nights
Sweet petrichor among bestrewn blossoms
Soothed the painted lashes of my heart

Thy sight led thorns to bloom
Yet turned spring covetous in gloom
Love-turned fangs slithered across
While clouds gave way for tides to cross

The prayer of a land that juddered
The yearning of a soul in blizzard
I shall enshrine thy for eternity in my heart
While seeking solace even when apart.

The Stolen Chamber

The citadel of my chambers
Turned to ruins at thy sight
For enamored I remained

Looking past the shoreline
Your presence draws the sun low
While it drowns timid

Approaching as do the wavelets
Crossing leagues in eons, with
Ceaseless throbbing awaiting thy warmth

For at thy presence shan't
The silver moon cast
Immuring hell within its ring

And etched in eternity ain't
Thy womb-like warmth in heart
Thy blossoming passion in mind
Thy infinite radiance in eyes
Thy soothing vocals capturing
Thy sweet innocence cradling souls across.

Sin Turned Kin

To thy is my soul
From womb to tomb
Wrapped in a mellifluous cloak
Thy warmth an eternal ecstasy

Blasphemy is thy existence
And nurturing is thy essence
A sin is thy presence
Yet thy spirit is all elegance.

An Eternal Vow

Of the entwined boughs with her beloved
And the enshrined vows with her other half
With ephemeral life turned eternal love
Lay the Stygian immured in prison.